50 Best Cheese Dishes

By: Kelly Johnson

Table of Contents

- Macaroni and Cheese
- Cheese Fondue
- Grilled Cheese Sandwich
- Cheese Pizza
- Cheeseburger
- Baked Brie
- Cheese Soufflé
- Cheese Quesadilla
- Caprese Salad
- Mozzarella Sticks
- Lasagna
- Cheese Enchiladas
- Cheese Stuffed Shells
- Cheesesteak Sandwich
- Four Cheese Pasta
- Cheese Omelette
- Pimento Cheese Spread

- Cheese-Stuffed Peppers
- Fettuccine Alfredo
- Blue Cheese Wedge Salad
- Paneer Tikka
- Cheese Grits
- Jalapeño Poppers
- Cheese and Charcuterie Board
- Broccoli Cheese Soup
- Cacio e Pepe
- Cheese Blintzes
- Cheese Empanadas
- Cheese Danish
- Cheese Straws
- Halloumi Fries
- Raclette
- Croque Monsieur
- Burrata with Tomatoes
- Cheese Tacos
- Queso Dip

- Spinach and Cheese Stuffed Chicken
- French Onion Soup with Gruyère
- Cheese Tamales
- Eggplant Parmesan
- Chili Cheese Fries
- Cheese-Stuffed Crust Pizza
- Cheese Gnocchi
- Cheesy Garlic Bread
- Cheese-Stuffed Meatballs
- Manicotti
- Baked Ziti
- Nachos with Cheese
- Cheddar Biscuits
- Cheese Ravioli

Macaroni and Cheese

Ingredients:

- 8 oz elbow macaroni
- 2 cups shredded cheddar cheese
- 2 cups milk
- 2 tbsp butter
- 2 tbsp flour
- Salt and pepper

Instructions:

1. Cook macaroni according to package instructions; drain.
2. In a saucepan, melt butter and whisk in flour to make a roux.
3. Slowly add milk, stirring constantly until thickened.
4. Stir in cheese until melted.
5. Mix cheese sauce with macaroni, season, and serve hot.

Cheese Fondue

Ingredients:

- 1 clove garlic, halved
- 1 cup dry white wine
- 8 oz Gruyère cheese, shredded
- 8 oz Emmental cheese, shredded
- 1 tsp lemon juice
- 1 tbsp cornstarch
- Bread cubes for dipping

Instructions:

1. Rub garlic inside a fondue pot.
2. Heat wine and lemon juice until hot, but not boiling.
3. Gradually add cheese, stirring until melted.
4. Mix cornstarch with a little water, add to cheese to thicken.
5. Keep warm and dip bread cubes.

Grilled Cheese Sandwich

Ingredients:

- 2 slices bread
- 2 slices cheddar or your favorite cheese
- Butter

Instructions:

1. Butter one side of each bread slice.
2. Place cheese between unbuttered sides.
3. Cook on skillet over medium heat until golden and cheese is melted, flipping once.

Cheese Pizza

Ingredients:

- Pizza dough
- 1 cup tomato sauce
- 2 cups shredded mozzarella
- Olive oil

Instructions:

1. Roll out dough, spread sauce evenly.
2. Sprinkle cheese on top.
3. Drizzle olive oil.
4. Bake at 475°F (245°C) for 12–15 minutes until crust is golden.

Cheeseburger

Ingredients:

- 1 lb ground beef
- Salt and pepper
- 4 slices cheddar cheese
- Burger buns
- Lettuce, tomato, pickles, condiments

Instructions:

1. Form beef into patties, season.
2. Grill or pan-fry to desired doneness.
3. Place cheese on patties near end to melt.
4. Assemble with buns and toppings.

Baked Brie

Ingredients:

- 1 wheel Brie cheese
- 2 tbsp honey or jam
- Nuts or dried fruit (optional)
- Crackers or sliced baguette

Instructions:

1. Place Brie on baking dish, drizzle honey or jam on top.
2. Add nuts or fruit if desired.
3. Bake at 350°F (175°C) for 10–15 minutes until soft.
4. Serve warm with crackers.

Cheese Soufflé

Ingredients:

- 3 tbsp butter
- 3 tbsp flour
- 1 cup milk
- 4 eggs, separated
- 1 ½ cups grated cheese (Gruyère or cheddar)
- Salt, pepper, pinch of nutmeg

Instructions:

1. Make a béchamel sauce with butter, flour, and milk.
2. Remove from heat, stir in cheese and egg yolks.
3. Beat egg whites until stiff peaks form, fold into cheese mixture.
4. Pour into buttered ramekins, bake at 375°F (190°C) for 25–30 mins until puffed and golden.

Cheese Quesadilla

Ingredients:

- 2 flour tortillas
- 1 ½ cups shredded cheese (cheddar, Monterey Jack)
- Optional: cooked chicken, veggies

Instructions:

1. Heat a tortilla in a skillet.
2. Sprinkle cheese evenly over tortilla, add extras if using.
3. Top with second tortilla.
4. Cook until cheese melts and tortilla is golden, flip once.
5. Cut into wedges and serve with salsa or sour cream.

Caprese Salad

Ingredients:

- Fresh mozzarella slices
- Ripe tomatoes, sliced
- Fresh basil leaves
- Olive oil
- Balsamic glaze
- Salt and pepper

Instructions:

1. Arrange alternating slices of mozzarella and tomato on a plate.
2. Tuck basil leaves between slices.
3. Drizzle with olive oil and balsamic glaze.
4. Season with salt and pepper.

Mozzarella Sticks

Ingredients:

- Mozzarella cheese sticks
- 1 cup flour
- 2 eggs, beaten
- 1 cup breadcrumbs
- Oil for frying

Instructions:

1. Coat cheese sticks in flour, then egg, then breadcrumbs. Repeat for a thicker crust if desired.
2. Freeze for at least 30 minutes to prevent melting.
3. Fry in hot oil until golden brown. Drain and serve with marinara sauce.

Lasagna

Ingredients:

- Lasagna noodles
- 2 cups ricotta cheese
- 2 cups shredded mozzarella
- 1 cup grated Parmesan
- 3 cups marinara sauce
- 1 lb ground beef or Italian sausage (optional)

Instructions:

1. Cook noodles. Brown meat if using.
2. Layer sauce, noodles, ricotta, meat, and mozzarella repeatedly.
3. Top with Parmesan and bake at 375°F (190°C) for 45 minutes.
4. Let rest before serving.

Cheese Enchiladas

Ingredients:

- Corn tortillas
- 2 cups shredded cheese (cheddar or Mexican blend)
- 1 cup enchilada sauce
- Sour cream and cilantro for garnish

Instructions:

1. Fill tortillas with cheese, roll, and place in baking dish.
2. Pour enchilada sauce over the top and sprinkle with more cheese.
3. Bake at 350°F (175°C) for 20 minutes.
4. Garnish with sour cream and cilantro.

Cheese Stuffed Shells

Ingredients:

- Jumbo pasta shells, cooked
- 2 cups ricotta cheese
- 1 cup shredded mozzarella
- 1 egg
- 2 cups marinara sauce

Instructions:

1. Mix ricotta, mozzarella, and egg.
2. Stuff shells with cheese mixture.
3. Place in baking dish with marinara sauce.
4. Bake at 375°F (190°C) for 30 minutes.

Cheesesteak Sandwich

Ingredients:

- Thinly sliced beef
- 1 onion, sliced
- 1 green bell pepper, sliced
- Provolone or American cheese
- Hoagie rolls

Instructions:

1. Sauté onions and peppers until soft.
2. Cook beef until browned.
3. Combine beef with veggies and cheese until melted.
4. Serve in hoagie rolls.

Four Cheese Pasta

Ingredients:

- 12 oz pasta
- ¼ cup Parmesan cheese
- ¼ cup mozzarella
- ¼ cup fontina cheese
- ¼ cup ricotta
- 1 cup cream or milk
- Salt and pepper

Instructions:

1. Cook pasta.
2. Heat cream, add cheeses gradually until melted and smooth.
3. Toss pasta with cheese sauce, season, and serve.

Cheese Omelette

Ingredients:

- 3 eggs
- ½ cup shredded cheese (cheddar, Swiss, or your choice)
- Salt and pepper
- Butter

Instructions:

1. Beat eggs with salt and pepper.
2. Melt butter in pan, pour eggs in.
3. When eggs begin to set, sprinkle cheese over half.
4. Fold omelette and cook until cheese melts.

Pimento Cheese Spread

Ingredients:

- 2 cups shredded cheddar cheese
- ½ cup mayonnaise
- 2 tbsp diced pimentos
- 1 tsp mustard
- Salt and pepper

Instructions:

1. Mix all ingredients until combined.
2. Chill before serving with crackers or bread.

Cheese-Stuffed Peppers

Ingredients:

- 4 large bell peppers
- 1 cup cooked rice
- 1 cup shredded cheese (cheddar or mozzarella)
- 1 cup cooked ground meat or beans (optional)
- 1 cup tomato sauce
- Salt and pepper

Instructions:

1. Preheat oven to 375°F (190°C).
2. Cut tops off peppers and remove seeds.
3. Mix rice, cheese, meat/beans, tomato sauce, salt, and pepper.
4. Stuff peppers with mixture and place in baking dish.
5. Cover with foil and bake for 30-35 minutes.

Fettuccine Alfredo

Ingredients:

- 12 oz fettuccine pasta
- 1 cup heavy cream
- ½ cup butter
- 1 cup grated Parmesan cheese
- Salt and pepper

Instructions:

1. Cook pasta and drain.
2. In a pan, melt butter and add cream, simmer briefly.
3. Stir in Parmesan until melted and sauce thickens.
4. Toss pasta with sauce, season, and serve immediately.

Blue Cheese Wedge Salad

Ingredients:

- Iceberg lettuce, cut into wedges
- Blue cheese dressing
- Crumbled blue cheese
- Bacon bits
- Cherry tomatoes, halved

Instructions:

1. Place wedge on plate.
2. Drizzle with blue cheese dressing.
3. Sprinkle crumbled cheese, bacon, and tomatoes on top.

Paneer Tikka

Ingredients:

- 250g paneer, cubed
- ½ cup yogurt
- 1 tbsp tikka masala spice mix
- 1 tbsp lemon juice
- Salt
- Bell peppers and onions (optional)

Instructions:

1. Mix yogurt, spices, lemon juice, and salt.
2. Marinate paneer and veggies in mixture for 1 hour.
3. Skewer and grill or bake at 400°F (200°C) for 15-20 minutes.

Cheese Grits

Ingredients:

- 1 cup grits
- 4 cups water or broth
- 1 cup shredded cheddar cheese
- 2 tbsp butter
- Salt and pepper

Instructions:

1. Bring water to boil, add grits slowly.
2. Cook stirring until thickened.
3. Stir in butter and cheese until melted.
4. Season to taste.

Jalapeño Poppers

Ingredients:

- 10 jalapeños, halved and seeded
- 1 cup cream cheese
- 1 cup shredded cheddar cheese
- 10 slices bacon (optional)

Instructions:

1. Mix cream cheese and cheddar.
2. Stuff jalapeño halves with cheese mixture.
3. Wrap with bacon if using.
4. Bake at 400°F (200°C) for 20 minutes or until bacon is crispy.

Cheese and Charcuterie Board

Ingredients:

- Variety of cheeses (brie, cheddar, gouda, blue)
- Assorted cured meats (salami, prosciutto)
- Crackers and bread
- Nuts, dried fruits, olives, fresh fruit

Instructions:

1. Arrange cheeses and meats on a large platter.
2. Add crackers, nuts, fruits around.
3. Serve at room temperature.

Broccoli Cheese Soup

Ingredients:

- 4 cups broccoli florets
- 1 cup chopped onions
- 4 cups chicken or vegetable broth
- 2 cups shredded cheddar cheese
- 1 cup milk or cream
- 3 tbsp butter
- 3 tbsp flour
- Salt and pepper

Instructions:

1. Sauté onions in butter until soft.
2. Stir in flour and cook 1-2 minutes.
3. Gradually whisk in broth and milk, bring to boil.
4. Add broccoli and simmer until tender.
5. Blend part of soup for texture if desired.
6. Stir in cheese until melted, season, and serve.

Cacio e Pepe

Ingredients:

- 12 oz spaghetti or tonnarelli
- 1 cup finely grated Pecorino Romano cheese
- 2 tsp freshly ground black pepper
- Salt
- Pasta cooking water

Instructions:

1. Cook pasta until al dente in salted water. Reserve 1 cup pasta water.
2. Toast black pepper in a dry pan to release aroma.
3. Drain pasta and add to pan with pepper.
4. Add grated cheese and some pasta water gradually, stirring vigorously to create a creamy sauce.
5. Adjust consistency with pasta water and serve immediately.

Cheese Blintzes

Ingredients:

- 1 cup flour
- 1 cup milk
- 2 eggs
- 1 cup ricotta or farmer's cheese
- 2 tbsp sugar
- Butter for frying
- Optional: sour cream and fruit preserves for serving

Instructions:

1. Make thin crepe batter with flour, milk, and eggs; cook thin pancakes.
2. Mix cheese with sugar.
3. Place a spoonful of cheese on each crepe, fold into a rectangular shape.
4. Fry in butter until golden on both sides.
5. Serve warm with sour cream and preserves.

Cheese Empanadas

Ingredients:

- Empanada dough (store-bought or homemade)
- 2 cups shredded cheese (cheddar, mozzarella, or mixed)
- 1 small onion, sautéed (optional)
- 1 egg for egg wash

Instructions:

1. Mix cheese and onion.
2. Roll out dough, cut into circles.
3. Place cheese filling on half of each circle, fold and seal edges.
4. Brush with egg wash.
5. Bake at 375°F (190°C) for 20-25 minutes or until golden.

Cheese Danish

Ingredients:

- Puff pastry sheets
- 1 cup cream cheese
- ¼ cup sugar
- 1 tsp vanilla extract
- 1 egg, beaten
- Optional: fruit jam for topping

Instructions:

1. Mix cream cheese, sugar, and vanilla.
2. Cut pastry into squares, place cheese mix in center.
3. Fold edges slightly, brush with egg.
4. Bake at 400°F (200°C) for 15-20 minutes.
5. Top with jam once cooled.

Cheese Straws

Ingredients:

- 1 cup shredded sharp cheddar cheese
- 1 cup flour
- ½ cup cold butter
- 1 tsp cayenne pepper (optional)
- Salt

Instructions:

1. Combine flour, cheese, butter, and seasoning to form dough.
2. Roll out and cut into strips.
3. Bake at 375°F (190°C) for 12-15 minutes until crispy.

Halloumi Fries

Ingredients:

- 1 block halloumi cheese, cut into fries
- Olive oil
- Lemon wedges for serving

Instructions:

1. Heat oil in a skillet.
2. Fry halloumi sticks until golden and crispy on all sides.
3. Drain and serve with lemon wedges.

Raclette

Ingredients:

- Raclette cheese slices
- Boiled baby potatoes
- Pickles and pickled onions
- Cured meats

Instructions:

1. Heat raclette cheese until melted (traditionally under a raclette grill).
2. Pour melted cheese over potatoes.
3. Serve with pickles and meats on the side.

Croque Monsieur

Ingredients:

- 8 slices white bread
- 4 slices ham
- 1 cup grated Gruyère or Swiss cheese
- 2 tbsp butter
- 2 tbsp flour
- 1 cup milk
- Dijon mustard

Instructions:

1. Make béchamel sauce: melt butter, whisk in flour, gradually add milk until thickened.
2. Spread mustard on bread slices.
3. Layer ham and cheese between bread slices.
4. Assemble sandwiches, top with béchamel and cheese.
5. Bake at 375°F (190°C) for 10-15 minutes until golden and bubbly.

Burrata with Tomatoes

Ingredients:

- 1 ball burrata cheese
- 2 cups cherry tomatoes, halved
- Fresh basil leaves
- Olive oil
- Salt and pepper
- Balsamic glaze (optional)

Instructions:

1. Arrange tomatoes on a plate and drizzle with olive oil.
2. Place burrata in the center.
3. Sprinkle salt, pepper, and fresh basil over.
4. Drizzle balsamic glaze if using. Serve immediately.

Cheese Tacos

Ingredients:

- Small corn or flour tortillas
- 1 cup shredded cheese (cheddar, Monterey Jack, or a blend)
- Optional: salsa, sour cream, guacamole, chopped cilantro

Instructions:

1. Warm tortillas in a skillet.
2. Sprinkle cheese on half of each tortilla, fold over.
3. Cook on both sides until cheese melts and tortilla is crispy.
4. Serve with desired toppings.

Queso Dip

Ingredients:

- 2 cups shredded white American cheese or Velveeta
- 1 cup diced tomatoes with green chilies
- ½ cup milk
- 1 tbsp butter
- 1 tsp chili powder (optional)

Instructions:

1. In a saucepan, melt butter.
2. Add milk and cheese, stirring until melted and smooth.
3. Stir in diced tomatoes and chili powder.
4. Serve warm with tortilla chips.

Spinach and Cheese Stuffed Chicken

Ingredients:

- 4 boneless chicken breasts
- 1 cup fresh spinach, chopped
- 1 cup shredded mozzarella or feta cheese
- 2 cloves garlic, minced
- Salt and pepper
- Olive oil

Instructions:

1. Preheat oven to 375°F (190°C).
2. Mix spinach, cheese, and garlic.
3. Cut a pocket in each chicken breast and stuff with the mixture.
4. Secure with toothpicks, season chicken with salt and pepper.
5. Heat oil in skillet, sear chicken on both sides.
6. Transfer to oven and bake 20-25 minutes until cooked through.

French Onion Soup with Gruyère

Ingredients:

- 4 large onions, thinly sliced
- 4 cups beef broth
- 2 tbsp butter
- 1 tbsp flour
- 1 cup Gruyère cheese, grated
- Baguette slices
- Salt and pepper

Instructions:

1. Sauté onions in butter over low heat until caramelized.
2. Stir in flour and cook 1-2 minutes.
3. Add beef broth, simmer 20 minutes.
4. Season with salt and pepper.
5. Ladle soup into oven-safe bowls, top with baguette slice and cheese.
6. Broil until cheese is bubbly and golden.

Cheese Tamales

Ingredients:

- Corn husks, soaked
- 2 cups masa harina
- 1 ½ cups chicken broth or water
- 1 cup shredded cheese (cheddar or Monterey Jack)
- ½ cup lard or vegetable shortening
- 1 tsp baking powder
- Salt

Instructions:

1. Beat lard until fluffy.
2. Mix masa harina, baking powder, and salt.
3. Add broth gradually and mix with lard until doughy.
4. Spread dough on soaked corn husks, add cheese in center.
5. Fold and steam tamales for 1 to 1.5 hours.

Eggplant Parmesan

Ingredients:

- 2 medium eggplants, sliced
- 2 cups marinara sauce
- 2 cups shredded mozzarella
- 1 cup grated Parmesan
- 2 eggs, beaten
- 1 cup breadcrumbs
- Olive oil
- Salt and pepper

Instructions:

1. Salt eggplant slices and let sit 30 mins, then rinse and pat dry.
2. Dip slices in egg, then breadcrumbs.
3. Fry in olive oil until golden.
4. Layer fried eggplant, marinara, mozzarella, and Parmesan in baking dish.
5. Bake at 375°F (190°C) for 25-30 minutes until bubbly.

Chili Cheese Fries

Ingredients:

- 4 cups cooked French fries
- 1 cup chili (with or without beans)
- 1 cup shredded cheddar cheese
- Sour cream and chopped green onions for topping

Instructions:

1. Spread fries on a baking sheet.
2. Spoon chili evenly over fries.
3. Sprinkle cheese on top.
4. Bake at 375°F (190°C) until cheese melts.
5. Top with sour cream and green onions.

Cheese-Stuffed Crust Pizza

Ingredients:

- Pizza dough
- 1 cup shredded mozzarella cheese (for crust)
- 1 ½ cups shredded mozzarella (for topping)
- Pizza sauce
- Toppings of choice (pepperoni, veggies, etc.)

Instructions:

1. Roll out dough into a circle.
2. Place string cheese or mozzarella sticks around edge, fold dough over and pinch to seal.
3. Spread pizza sauce on center.
4. Add cheese and toppings.
5. Bake at 475°F (245°C) for 12-15 minutes until crust is golden and cheese is melted.

Cheese Gnocchi

Ingredients:

- 2 cups ricotta cheese
- 1 egg
- 1 cup grated Parmesan cheese
- 1 cup flour
- Salt and pepper

Instructions:

1. Mix ricotta, egg, Parmesan, salt, and pepper.
2. Gradually add flour to form a soft dough.
3. Roll dough into ropes, cut into 1-inch pieces.
4. Boil gnocchi until they float, then drain.
5. Serve with your favorite sauce.

Cheesy Garlic Bread

Ingredients:

- 1 baguette or Italian bread
- ½ cup butter, softened
- 3 cloves garlic, minced
- 1 ½ cups shredded mozzarella cheese
- 2 tbsp chopped parsley

Instructions:

1. Preheat oven to 375°F (190°C).
2. Mix butter and garlic.
3. Slice bread in half lengthwise and spread garlic butter.
4. Top with cheese and parsley.
5. Bake 10-12 minutes until cheese is melted and bubbly.

Cheese-Stuffed Meatballs

Ingredients:

- 1 lb ground beef or turkey
- 1 cup shredded mozzarella
- ½ cup breadcrumbs
- 1 egg
- 2 cloves garlic, minced
- Salt and pepper
- Marinara sauce

Instructions:

1. Mix beef, breadcrumbs, egg, garlic, salt, and pepper.
2. Form small patties, place cheese in center, then cover with more meat and shape into balls.
3. Bake at 400°F (200°C) for 20 minutes or until cooked through.
4. Serve with marinara sauce.

Manicotti

Ingredients:

- 8 manicotti pasta shells, cooked
- 2 cups ricotta cheese
- 1 cup shredded mozzarella
- 1 cup grated Parmesan
- 1 egg
- 2 cups marinara sauce

Instructions:

1. Mix ricotta, mozzarella, Parmesan, and egg.
2. Stuff cooked manicotti shells with cheese mixture.
3. Spread marinara sauce in baking dish, place manicotti on top, cover with more sauce.
4. Bake at 350°F (175°C) for 30 minutes.
5. Top with extra cheese if desired.

Baked Ziti

Ingredients:

- 1 lb ziti pasta, cooked
- 2 cups marinara sauce
- 2 cups shredded mozzarella
- 1 cup ricotta cheese
- ½ cup grated Parmesan

Instructions:

1. Mix pasta with marinara and ricotta.
2. Pour into baking dish, top with mozzarella and Parmesan.
3. Bake at 375°F (190°C) for 25-30 minutes until bubbly.

Nachos with Cheese

Ingredients:

- Tortilla chips
- 2 cups shredded cheddar cheese
- Optional: jalapeños, black olives, diced tomatoes, sour cream, guacamole

Instructions:

1. Spread chips on a baking sheet.
2. Sprinkle cheese and toppings.
3. Bake at 375°F (190°C) for 10 minutes or until cheese melts.
4. Serve with sour cream and guacamole.

Cheddar Biscuits

Ingredients:

- 2 cups all-purpose flour
- 1 tbsp baking powder
- ½ tsp salt
- ½ cup cold butter, cubed
- 1 cup shredded cheddar cheese
- ¾ cup milk

Instructions:

1. Preheat oven to 425°F (220°C).
2. Mix flour, baking powder, salt.
3. Cut in butter until crumbly.
4. Stir in cheese, then add milk to form dough.
5. Drop dough onto baking sheet and bake 12-15 minutes.

Cheese Ravioli

Ingredients:

- Fresh pasta dough or store-bought sheets
- 2 cups ricotta cheese
- 1 cup grated Parmesan
- 1 egg
- Salt and pepper
- Marinara or butter sauce

Instructions:

1. Mix ricotta, Parmesan, egg, salt, and pepper.
2. Roll out pasta dough, place small spoonfuls of cheese mixture spaced apart.
3. Cover with another pasta sheet, press around filling, cut into squares.
4. Boil ravioli 3-4 minutes until they float.
5. Serve with sauce.

www.ingramcontent.com/pod-product-compliance
Lightning Source LLC
LaVergne TN
LVHW081323060526
838201LV00055B/2429